THIS BOOK BELONGS TO:

Golden Age Press

VISIT US ONLINE:
WWW.GOLDENAGEPRESS.COM

ISBN-13 : 978-1955421560

Illustrated by: Roslen Roy Mack

More fun coming your way!

visit us at goldenagepress.com/horse-cb

Join our newsletter and be the first to know about our new releases, + get free coloring pages to encourage their creativity and imagination.

Cute Cats

Coloring Book for Kids
Ages 4-8

DINOSAUR
Coloring Book

Ages 4-8

Cute Dogs

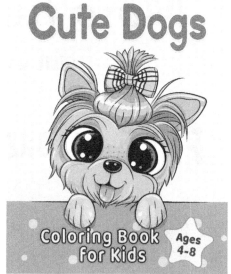

Coloring Book for Kids
Ages 4-8

Unicorn
Coloring Book

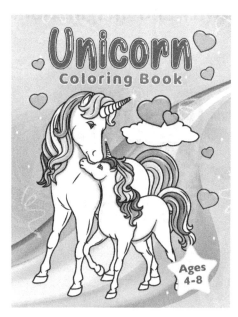

Ages 4-8

Christmas
Coloring Book for Kids

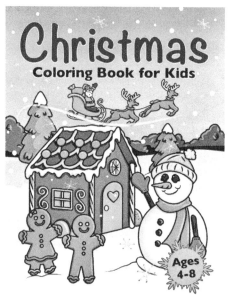

Ages 4-8

Ocean
Coloring Book

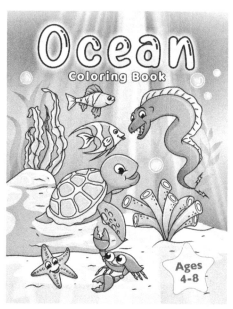

Ages 4-8

EASTER
Coloring Book for Kids

Ages 4-8

TODDLER HALLOWEEN
COLORING BOOK

AGES 2-4

Cute Owls

Coloring Book for Kids
Ages 4-8

More Fun Titles Available!

USA

CANADA

UNITED
KINGDOM

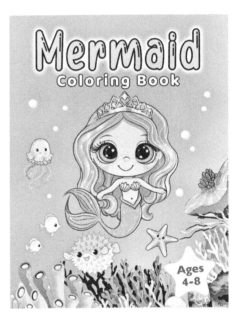

We're always
releasing new
books so be
sure to check
back often!

Made in the USA
Monee, IL
21 December 2022

23333616R00037